The Heart of Broken People

Finding Hope and Healing in the Depths of Despair

By

Abhishek H Rathod

The Heart of Broken People
©Copyright 2024-2025 Abhishek H Rathod, The Heart of
Broken People

ISBN: 9798896 102168, 9798896 102175

Expanded Edition

Notion Press, Inc.

800, West El Camino Real #180,

California USA 94040

Notion Press Media Pvt Ltd,

#7 Red Cross Road,

Egmore, Chennai, Tamil Nadu 600008

Email Id: publish@notionpress.com

Abhishek Rathod Contact : Rabhendra@gmail.com

Phone Number : +91 8128497582

CONTENTS

ABOUT THE AUTHOR

Abhendra Rathod

Abhishek Hareshkumar Rathod, better known as Abhendra Rathod, is a passionate artist whose journey began on December 1, 1998, in Idar, Gujarat. Growing up in the small village of Chithoda in the Vijaynagar Taluka of Sabarkantha district, he was inspired by the vibrant stories and emotions that surrounded him.

Education and Career

Abhendra graduated with a B.Sc. in Microbiology and went on to complete a Certificate Course of Medical Laboratory Technician (PG.CMLT). He landed a position at GMERS Medical College in Himatnagar, where he gained invaluable experience and insights into the medical field, deepening his understanding of life and human experiences. After two years he resigned to pursue his true passions in music and writing.

Musical Journey

In addition to his academic achievements, Abhendra has pursued his passion for music as a singer-songwriter. His debut book, **THE HEART OF BROKEN PEOPLE**, showcases his ability to weave themes of love, loss, and healing into compelling narratives. Through his music and writing, he invites readers to explore their own journeys of heartache and hope.

Creative Pursuits

Abhendra's talents don't stop at music and writing. He has completed courses in vocal training and mixing/mastering, further enhancing his musical abilities. He is also skilled in content creation, photo and video editing. His work has been featured in several Indian and international magazines, including Artega, Figgi, TopPoster, and Musical Satan. Currently, he is exploring opportunities in modeling, showcasing yet another facet of his artistic identity.

Vision and Future

With this first literary endeavor, Abhendra aims to connect with readers on a deeper level, emphasizing that art—in all its forms—has the power to heal and inspire. His journey is just beginning, and he is eager to share his stories and experiences with the world, reminding us all of the beauty that can emerge from heartache.

Author Name
Abhishek H Rathod

FOREWORD

A Journey Through Heartbreak

In a world where love often takes canter stage, the stories of heartbreak and resilience frequently go unheard. **THE HEART OF BROKEN PEOPLE** offers a poignant exploration of this often-overlooked aspect of the human experience. Abhendra Rathod, in his debut literary work, invites us to journey through the complex emotions of love, loss, and the healing process that follows.

A Lyrical Exploration

Abhendra's background as a singer-songwriter infuses this book with a lyrical quality, capturing the rawness of emotion in a way that resonates deeply. His narratives are not just tales of sorrow; they are reflections of our collective struggles and triumphs. Each chapter serves as a testament to the resilience of the human spirit, showing us that even in our darkest moments, there is a flicker of hope waiting to be discovered.

Finding Yourself in the Stories

As you turn the pages, you will encounter characters who face the depths of despair and emerge transformed. You'll witness their struggles and triumphs, and in their stories, you may find pieces of your own journey. This book encourages us to embrace our vulnerabilities, recognizing that they are integral to our growth and healing.

Relatable and Moving

Abhendra's ability to blend personal experiences with universal themes makes this work not just relatable but deeply moving. His exploration of one-sided love, tragic relationships, and the quest for self-identity will resonate with anyone who has ever loved and lost.

Embracing Resilience

As you delve into **THE HEART OF BROKEN PEOPLE**, prepare to embark on a transformative journey—one that celebrates the beauty of resilience and the power of love, even in its most painful forms. Abhendra Rathod has crafted a beautiful ode to the broken, reminding us that from heartache can arise the most profound forms of healing and renewal.

[Abhishek H Rathod]
[Artist/Writer]
[2024]

The Heart of Broken People

Finding Hope and Healing in the Depths of Despair

INTRODUCTION

Welcome to *THE HEART OF BROKEN PEOPLE*, a journey into the complexities of love, heartbreak, and the intricate webs we weave in our relationships. This book delves deep into the emotional landscapes that shape us, especially when love feels one-sided or tragically lost.

At its core, this story follows Abhendra and Isha, two souls navigating the turbulent waters of college life, friendship, and unspoken desires. Abhendra, a talented artist and top student, grapples with his introverted nature and the weight of expectations. He is admired for his mysterious aura and artistic flair, yet he finds himself haunted by anxiety and a longing for connection. On the other hand, Isha is a spirited dreamer, ambitious and clever, who yearns to escape her small-town life and make a mark on the world. Her desire for attention and validation often leads her into a complex dance of flirtation with Abhendra, leaving both of them in a constant state of confusion.

Through their eyes, we explore themes of heartbreak, fear of rejection, and the struggle for authenticity in a world that often prioritizes appearances over genuine connection. The juxtaposition of their desires and fears creates a narrative that resonates with anyone who has ever felt trapped in a cycle of longing, insecurity, and unreciprocated feelings.

As you turn the pages, prepare to dive into the depths of their hearts, witness the struggles they face, and discover the power of vulnerability and self-acceptance. *THE HEART OF THE BROKEN PEOPLE* is not just a story about love; it's a reflection of the human experience, revealing that even in our brokenness, there is room for rebirth and transformation.

Join Abhendra and Isha on their journey as they seek to find themselves amidst the chaos of emotions, and ultimately, learn what it truly means to love and be loved.

"Every broken heart has a story, and this is mine." – Abhendra Rathod

CHAPTER 1: STUCK

Introduction to Abhendra and Isha

Abhendra woke to the blaring of his alarm, its shrill sound cutting through the fog of a restless night. As he lay in bed, staring at the ceiling, a familiar heaviness settled in his chest. Each day felt like a repeat of the last, filled with unspoken feelings and the burdens of anxiety. It was just another day to navigate through the emotional haze that seemed to engulf him.

Two years ago, everything changed on college admission day. The campus buzzed with excitement, a cacophony of nervous chatter and hopeful dreams. Amid the throngs of students, Abhendra caught sight of Isha. Her bright smile and quick wit made her stand out, drawing him in like a moth to a flame. From that moment, something clicked; he felt an undeniable connection.

The Spark of Connection

Isha was everything he admired—ambitious, clever, and always dreaming of studying abroad. She spun tales of adventure that sparkled in her eyes, and Abhendra found himself captivated by her charisma. Yet beneath her playful exterior lay a complexity that both intrigued and unsettled him. Her tendency to exaggerate made him question the authenticity of her words, but instead of confronting her, he indulged in her fantasies, enthralled by her unpredictability.

Despite being the class topper in microbiology, Abhendra was introverted by nature. He excelled academically, driven by a desire to prove himself, but the spotlight often felt suffocating. His achievements brought admiration, yet with it came the weight of expectations. He was also a multi-talented artist—a singer-songwriter with a growing social media following—but he often preferred the solace of his own thoughts to the clamor of social interactions. The fear of not being good enough and of failing to meet others' expectations loomed over him like a dark cloud, overshadowing his accomplishments.

In their lecture hall, Isha claimed the second bench, a perfect spot for stealing glances at Abhendra without drawing attention. But today was different. She was drawing more attention than usual, playfully interacting with her friends while glancing at him, creating an atmosphere charged with flirtation and intrigue. Her laughter rang out, and her animated gestures seemed designed to capture the attention of everyone around, especially Abhendra. He couldn't help but feel that she relished the spotlight, wanting to showcase their connection as something more than just friendship.

Abhendra hated this attention. It made him uncomfortable, and he found himself wishing she wouldn't flirt so openly. It felt like she was playing a game, flaunting their relationship to draw more eyes, more admiration. Did she truly care for him, or was he merely a pawn in her desire for social status? He wanted their bond to be genuine, free from the theatrics that surrounded them, but Isha seemed to thrive on the attention.

Rolling out of bed, he went through his morning routine, but everything felt heavier than usual. Brushing his teeth, washing his face—these mundane tasks felt monumental against the backdrop of his inner turmoil. He caught his reflection in the mirror; the tired eyes staring back held a mixture of confusion and longing. Who was he, really? A high-achieving student? A talented artist? Or a boy trapped in unrequited love?

At college, the laughter of his classmates echoed around him, a stark contrast to the storm brewing inside. He could hear them discussing weekend plans, sharing stories, but all he could think about was Isha. She texted him throughout the day, weaving playful banter into their conversations, yet he couldn't shake the feeling that he was stuck in a cycle of one-sided love. What if she didn't see him the way he saw her? What if her affections were merely a game, a diversion from her reality?

As the hours dragged on, anticipation gnawed at him. Finally, mid-morning, his phone buzzed with a message from Isha. "Hey! You free later? Want to grab coffee?" The thrill of her message sent a jolt through him, a mix of excitement and dread. The café they frequented had become a refuge, but it also served as a battleground for his emotions. He could already envision their usual spot, the warm ambiance, the aroma of freshly brewed coffee, but he also felt the weight of uncertainty that came with it.

After a moment of hesitation, he replied, "Sure, what time?" The words felt like both an invitation and a trap—an acceptance of the cycle he was trapped in, promising hope yet delivering only heartache.

As the day wore on, he tried to focus on his studies, but his mind was a whirlwind of thoughts. Memories of their shared laughter and deep conversations flooded his mind—the way Isha leaned closer during lectures, the playful jabs they exchanged, and the warmth of her presence that felt like home. Yet doubts crept in, reminding him of the barriers that lay between them. What if she didn't feel the same? What if her flirtation was simply a mask for her own insecurities?

Finally, the clock struck five, and he found himself walking to the café. Each step felt heavier, as though he were dragging the weight of his insecurities along with him. When he entered, Isha was already there, sitting at their usual table, her smile radiating warmth. For a moment, his heart soared, but as he approached, anxiety settled back in, tightening its grip.

"Hey! You made it!" she exclaimed, her eyes sparkling with mischief.

"Of course," he replied, forcing a smile as he sat down. The familiar comfort of her presence felt both inviting and suffocating, a paradox he struggled to understand.

"Did you hear about the new exchange program? I'm thinking of applying!" she said, leaning forward, her excitement infectious.

"Really? You've mentioned that before," he said, trying to keep his tone light. "Do you think you'll actually go through with it this time?"

Isha laughed, brushing off his skepticism. "Oh, come on! You know I'm just a dreamer. Who wouldn't want to explore the world?"

As they talked, Abhendra felt her playfulness drawing attention from nearby tables. A few classmates snickered and whispered, casting sidelong glances in their direction. It was as if Isha was showcasing their relationship, basking in the intrigue she generated. The realization stung. Did she want to hype herself up through him?

He felt a knot tightening in his stomach. "Isha, do you really need to play it up like this?" he blurted out, unable to mask his discomfort.

She raised an eyebrow, her playful demeanor faltering. "What do you mean?"

"I don't know, it just feels like you're putting on a show," he said, his voice softer now, almost pleading. "I want us to be real, not just... an act for everyone to see."

Her expression shifted, surprise mingling with frustration. "I'm not acting! I just like having fun. Is that such a crime?"

Abhendra sighed, rubbing the back of his neck. "It's not a crime, but I wish it didn't feel like a performance. Can't we just be ourselves?"

For a moment, silence hung between them, thick with unspoken tension. Isha looked away, and he could see the wheels turning in her mind. She wanted to tell him how much she loved him, but the fear of rejection loomed large, just as it did for him.

"Maybe I just like the attention," she said finally, her voice barely above a whisper. "It's hard not to when you're as popular as you are."

Abhendra's heart sank. He understood the allure of wanting to be recognized, especially when standing next to someone like him. But that realization made him feel even more trapped. He had always hoped that their connection was deeper than superficial admiration. Did she really care about him, or was he just another notch in her belt, another way to gain clout?

"I just... I want to know you, Isha. Not just this version everyone else sees," he confessed, his voice cracking slightly. "It's hard for me to navigate all of this."

Her eyes softened, a flicker of understanding passing between them. "I know. I just thought... maybe if I acted like I had it all together, you'd see me differently. Like I could impress you."

Abhendra felt a wave of empathy wash over him. They were both navigating this emotional landscape, trying to hide their insecurities behind layers of bravado. He wanted to reach out, to assure her that he admired her for more than her social status. But a part of him still hesitated, tethered by his own fears.

"Maybe we should just be honest with each other," he suggested gently, hoping to bridge the chasm that lay between them.

"Yeah, maybe," she replied, her tone contemplative. "But it's hard. I'm not used to being vulnerable."

"Neither am I," he admitted, feeling a strange sense of solidarity.

As they wrapped up their coffee, the conversation lingered in the air, heavy with unspoken possibilities. Abhendra couldn't shake the feeling of being stuck— caught in a cycle of unrequited love and anxiety, unsure of how to escape. He took a deep breath, the weight of his heart heavy in his chest, and made his way home, feeling as if he were wandering through a haze of despair.

The shadows of his past loomed large, and the familiar voice of anxiety whispered doubts in his ear. Memories flooded back—moments when he had felt truly powerful, commanding the stage with his music, pouring his soul into every note. Yet those moments were now eclipsed by his feelings for Isha.

He longed for the confidence he felt when performing, but in her presence, he felt fragmented.

"Sometimes, the hardest part of moving forward is accepting where you are."

–Abhendra Rathod

CHAPTER:2 HOPE

Moments of Friendship and Confusion

The sun rose the next day, casting a warm glow over the campus, but Abhendra felt the familiar weight of uncertainty pressing down on him. He replayed his conversation with Isha in his mind, trying to make sense of the tangled emotions they both shared. As he walked through the bustling corridors, the laughter and chatter of students filled the air, but his heart felt heavy, stuck between hope and doubt.

When he arrived in class, he spotted Isha sitting on the second bench, her sketchbook open in front of her. Today, she seemed lost in her art, her brow furrowed in concentration. He felt a flutter in his chest—she looked beautiful when she focused. But as he took his seat, the memories of their last encounter haunted him.

Isha glanced up and caught his gaze, her expression shifting from concentration to a bright smile that made his heart race. "Hey, stranger!" she called, her voice cheerful, as if nothing had happened between them.

"Hey," he replied, trying to smile back, but it felt a bit forced.

As the lecture began, Abhendra struggled to focus. His thoughts drifted back to Isha's laughter and the way she effortlessly drew attention. It both intrigued and frustrated him. Why did she need to be so dramatic? Couldn't they just be themselves?

Halfway through the class, Isha turned to him, her eyes sparkling. "So, are we still friends after my 'performance' yesterday?"

Her teasing tone made him chuckle. "I guess so, but I still think you love the attention a bit too much."

Isha feigned shock, placing a hand over her heart. "Me? Never! I just like to keep things interesting. Besides, you're the popular one here!"

"Popular?" He raised an eyebrow. "It feels more like you're putting on a show."

She laughed, her eyes bright. "Okay, maybe I do enjoy a little spotlight. But only because it's fun! I want people to see that I can be more than just the quiet girl."

Abhendra leaned back, intrigued by her openness. "I get that. But isn't it exhausting to keep up an act?"

"Sometimes," she admitted, her smile fading slightly. "But I feel like I have to prove something, especially to myself. If I don't take risks, how will I stand out?"

Her words resonated with him. He understood the desire to be seen, to be recognized for one's worth. "I get it, but there's strength in being real. You don't have to be perfect to impress anyone."

She looked at him thoughtfully. "Maybe you're right. It's just hard to show who I really am."

Their conversation was interrupted by the professor, pulling them back into the lecture. Abhendra scribbled notes but couldn't help glancing at Isha. She was focused again, and he wondered what she was really thinking. Beneath her playful exterior, there was a depth he wanted to explore.

After class, as they gathered their things, Abhendra hesitated. "Hey, do you want to grab lunch? Just us?"

Isha's face lit up. "Absolutely! I'd love to."

As they walked to the cafeteria, the conversation flowed easily. They joked about classes, shared stories from childhood, and discussed their favorite music. For the first time, Abhendra felt a spark of hope. Maybe their relationship could be more than just an act.

In the cafeteria, they found a cozy corner table. Over sandwiches and fries, the atmosphere shifted. Isha's voice grew quieter. "You know, I've been thinking about what you said. About being real."

Abhendra leaned in, eager to hear more. "And?"

"I guess I've been afraid," she admitted, looking down at her food. "Afraid that if I show who I really am, people won't like me. But I want to try."

Admiration surged in him. "That's brave, Isha. It's not easy to be open."

"I know," she replied, her gaze steady. "But you make it easier. You're so genuine, Abhendra. I really admire that about you."

His heart raced at her words. "Thank you. I've struggled with being genuine, too. I guess we're both trying to figure things out."

The conversation shifted back to lighter topics, but the undercurrent of honesty lingered. As they finished lunch, Isha looked thoughtful. "What if we made a pact? To be more open with each other? No more games, just us?"

He felt a rush of excitement. "I'd like that. It's a deal."

The Struggle to Express Emotions

After lunch, as they walked back to class, Abhendra felt a lightness he hadn't experienced in a while. Hope flickered in his heart—a feeling that they could move beyond uncertainty and truly connect.

Yet, even amidst this budding hope, Abhendra sensed something was off. Isha's playful flirtation sometimes felt more like a performance than genuine affection. He caught glimpses of her vulnerability, but there were moments when he felt walls around her heart. Did she genuinely like him, or was she drawn to his popularity? It nagged at him, but he pushed those thoughts aside. Instead, he focused on the positive—the moments they shared that felt real.

As the days unfolded, he embraced this hope. Each conversation with Isha brought him closer to breaking free from his past. With every laugh and moment of honesty, he felt lighter, shedding layers of doubt and insecurity.

Still, he wondered who Isha truly was beneath her layers. Could he trust her with his heart? But more importantly, he realized he was on a journey to find himself. Being stuck didn't have to mean being lost; it could also mean discovering who he truly was, separate from his past.

In this emotional journey, Abhendra found something surprising within himself—a determination to dig deeper, not just into Isha's heart, but into his own. He wanted to confront the parts of himself that felt afraid and to dismantle the walls he had built from years of anxiety and self-doubt.

As he and Isha continued to navigate their relationship, he began to see flickers of hope in his mind—small lights illuminating the darkness of his past. With Isha, he felt invigorated by the possibility of growth and healing. In opening up to her, he found not only her heart but also the courage to confront his own.

Ready to discover what lay ahead, he embraced this journey, determined to find himself amidst the complexities of connection, vulnerability, and the fragile hope of love

""Hope is the quiet voice that whispers, 'Try again,' when everything else screams 'Give up.'"
– Abhendra Rathod

CHAPTER:3 SAD

The Turning Point of Their Relationship

As the days passed, the air around Abhendra and Isha felt heavier, weighed down by unspoken thoughts and lingering doubts. What had begun as a lighthearted connection now felt complicated, and Abhendra found himself grappling with a growing sadness he couldn't shake off. He watched Isha navigate her emotions, the sparkle in her eyes often dimmed by something deeper.

One afternoon, they sat in a quiet corner of the campus, the sun casting gentle shadows on the grass. Isha was sketching, her pencil moving swiftly across the page, but Abhendra noticed how her usual enthusiasm seemed absent. "Hey, Isha," he said, breaking the silence. "Are you okay?"

She paused, biting her lip, and looked up at him. "Yeah, just... lost in thought, I guess."

He shifted closer, sensing something was off. "You can talk to me, you know. If something's bothering you."

She hesitated, her gaze drifting to the ground. "It's just... sometimes I feel so overwhelmed. I have all these dreams, but I don't know how to reach them. And I don't want to let anyone down."

Abhendra's heart ached for her. "I get that. It's hard to chase your dreams, especially when it feels like there are so many obstacles."

Isha sighed, running a hand through her hair. "And then there's the pressure to be perfect. To be the fun, carefree girl everyone expects me to be. But inside, I feel like I'm struggling."

The vulnerability in her voice pierced through the lightness they usually shared. Abhendra wanted to reassure her, to lift her spirits, but he could sense the weight of her sadness. "You don't have to put on a show for me, Isha. I like you for who you are, not who you pretend to be."

Tears brimmed in her eyes, and she looked away, afraid to let them fall. "It's just hard to be real when I'm so afraid of being judged. I feel like I'm constantly trying to live up to everyone's expectations."

"Maybe you need to let go of those expectations," he said gently. "You're allowed to be yourself, even if that means showing your struggles."

"But what if I show you my real self and it's not enough?" she whispered, her voice shaking.

Abhendra reached out, placing his hand over hers. "You are more than enough, Isha. No matter what you think, I'm here for you. I want to see all of you, even the messy parts."

For a moment, they sat in silence, the weight of their conversation hanging in the air. Isha finally took a deep breath, a flicker of determination lighting her eyes. "Okay. I'll try to be more open. But it's scary."

"I know," he replied. "But we can face it together. I'm scared too, you know. I have my own fears and anxieties."

As he spoke, a sense of hope began to stir within him. Maybe this shared vulnerability could be the key to breaking through the sadness that hung over them. Abhendra felt lighter, knowing they were both willing to confront their struggles.

"I've always wanted to go abroad to chase my dreams," Isha said, her voice gaining strength. "But I've held back because I'm scared of failing. I don't want to disappoint anyone, especially myself."

Abhendra nodded, his heart aching for her. "It's okay to be afraid. But what if you took that fear and turned it into motivation? You deserve to pursue what makes you happy."

A small smile tugged at her lips. "You really think so?"

"I do," he replied earnestly. "And I'll be here to support you, no matter what. We can tackle our dreams together."

As they talked, the sun dipped lower in the sky, casting a warm glow around them. Abhendra felt a shift, a lightness breaking through the sadness. Isha's honesty sparked a new connection between them, allowing them to share their fears without judgment.

That day marked a turning point for both of them. Abhendra realized that sadness could coexist with hope, that it was okay to feel lost sometimes. Together, they began to embrace their vulnerabilities, learning that opening up to each other was a strength, not a weakness.

The Impact of Their Choices

But as the festival of Navratri approached, everything changed. Isha started to withdraw completely. She became quieter, often lost in her own world. When Abhendra reached out with messages, she responded less frequently. The spark that once lit their conversations now felt dimmed, replaced by a distant sadness he couldn't understand.

"Hey, is everything okay?" he texted one evening, his heart racing as he hit send.

Minutes turned into hours, but there was no response. Each unanswered message felt like a weight pressing down on him. The silence gnawed at him, and he told himself she might just be busy with the festivities. Yet, as days passed with no communication, he couldn't shake the feeling that something was seriously wrong.

During the Navratri celebrations, Abhendra noticed Isha surrounded by other friends, laughing and chatting animatedly. They shared smiles, inside jokes, and moments that seemed to exclude him entirely. The sight hurt more than he expected. He felt invisible, like a shadow lingering at the edges of their joy. It stung to see her vibrant with others while he felt increasingly isolated.

Every day was a struggle. Abhendra fought the rising sadness that came with the realization that Isha might be using him as a temporary comfort, only to discard him when things got tough. The thought of being ignored, of feeling used, churned in his stomach. Did she ever really care about him, or was he just a passing phase in her life?

As he walked through the campus, he couldn't help but get lost in his thoughts. He imagined their conversations, the laughter they shared, the way she had looked at him with such warmth. But those moments felt like they were fading, replaced by a harsh reality where he felt alone. He started to question everything—what had gone wrong? Had he misread her feelings? Did she only enjoy his company when it was convenient?

Abhendra poured his frustration into his art, using music as a release for the emotions he couldn't articulate. Late at night, he found solace in writing songs that expressed his heartache, channeling his feelings of rejection and longing into melodies that resonated with his pain.

Still, he held onto a flicker of hope that maybe Isha would reach out. But as the days turned into a blur, that hope dimmed, leaving him trapped in a cycle of sadness and imagination. He yearned for the connection they once had but feared that it was slipping away forever.

In his heart, he knew he had to confront this feeling of being used, to understand what was happening between them. But with each passing day, the distance between them seemed to grow wider, leaving Abhendra feeling more stuck than ever, caught in a web of his own imagination and uncertainty.

"Sadness isn't the absence of joy; it's the depth of what you once had."

– Abhendra Rathod

CHAPTER:4 OH, LORD TAKE THIS PAIN AWAY

Isha's Family Pressures

The air around Abhendra felt thick with sorrow as the days of Navratri dragged on. He watched Isha from a distance, surrounded by friends and laughter, her radiant smile a stark contrast to the turmoil in his heart. Each day, he fought the urge to reach out, to break through the wall she had built around herself. Instead, he found himself drifting through his college life, a mere spectator in a play where he once held a leading role.

With every passing moment, he felt the weight of his emotions pressing down on him. The loneliness wrapped around him like a heavy cloak, suffocating yet familiar. He tried to focus on his studies and engage with friends who reached out to him, but his thoughts always returned to Isha. Why was she shutting him out? Did she even realize how much her silence affected him?

One evening, after another long day of pretending everything was okay, Abhendra returned to his small apartment, the silence echoing around him. He dropped his backpack on the floor and sank into a chair, staring blankly at the wall. Thoughts swirled in his mind—

memories of their laughter, the way she had looked at him, and the connection they had shared. It all felt so distant now, like a beautiful dream he had awoken from too soon.

"Why is this happening?" he whispered to the empty room. "Why does it hurt so much?"

In search of solace, he turned to music, his refuge in times of despair. He picked up his guitar, fingers trembling as they brushed over the strings. The familiar sensation of the instrument grounded him, offering a fragile sense of comfort. He began to play, pouring his heart into the notes, allowing the melodies to convey the pain he struggled to express in words.

As he played, lyrics began to flow from his heart:

Every heartbeat, tied to you alone,

But you never cared, left me on my own.

I loved you deeply, you never saw me,

Oh Lord, take this pain away, set my heart free.

He closed his eyes, letting the music wrap around him like a warm embrace. It was in these moments that he felt a semblance of release, as if the strings of his guitar could carry away some of the heaviness he felt within.

Hours passed, and he lost track of time, immersed in his music. The world outside faded away, replaced by the raw emotions pouring from his heart. Each strum brought clarity, allowing him to process the chaos swirling in his mind.

But as the song concluded, the silence crept back in, bringing with it the bitter taste of reality. Isha was still out there, laughing and living her life while he felt like a ghost haunting the corners of their shared memories. The thought twisted in his gut, and he wondered if she had truly moved on or if she was merely hiding behind a façade.

The next morning, Abhendra made a decision. He couldn't continue like this, lost in his own suffering while Isha remained a mystery. He needed to confront his feelings and find a way to understand what was happening between them.

As he walked through the campus, he gathered his courage, determined to speak to her. The festival was in full swing, and vibrant decorations adorned every corner. Music filled the air, and the atmosphere was alive with energy. But for Abhendra, everything felt muted. He searched for Isha amidst the crowd, his heart racing with anxiety.

Finally, he spotted her near the entrance, chatting animatedly with a group of friends. She looked radiant, her laughter ringing like music. He hesitated, his mind racing with doubts. Would she even want to talk to him? Would she push him away again?

Summoning every ounce of courage, he approached her, his heart pounding in his chest. "Isha," he called softly.

She turned, her eyes widening in surprise. "Abhendra!" For a fleeting moment, her expression flickered with warmth, but it quickly vanished, replaced by a guarded look. "Hey."

He felt a pang of disappointment at her response. "Can we talk?"

"Sure, but I'm a bit busy right now," she replied, glancing back at her friends, who were already pulling her into conversation.

"I just need a moment," he insisted, desperation creeping into his voice.

Isha's smile faltered, and she nodded hesitantly, stepping away from her friends. "Okay, just for a minute."

They moved to a quieter corner, the noise of the festivities fading into the background. Abhendra took a deep breath, searching for the right words. "I've been worried about you. You've been… distant lately."

Her gaze dropped, and for a moment, he saw vulnerability flicker in her eyes. "I know. I've just been dealing with a lot of things."

"What kind of things?" he pressed gently. "You can talk to me, Isha. I'm here for you."

She looked up, a mix of frustration and sadness etched across her face. "It's complicated, Abhendra. I have so many expectations on me, and I'm scared of failing. I don't want to burden you with my problems."

Her words struck him with a painful clarity. He realized that Isha was not just battling her internal demons but also the immense pressure from her family. They had dreams for her—career aspirations, academic achievements, and social expectations. Each of those burdens added weight to her already heavy heart. Abhendra wished he could help lighten that load, but it seemed she was determined to carry it alone.

His heart sank. "You're not a burden. I care about you. I just want to understand what's going on."

Isha took a step back, her walls going up once more. "I appreciate that, but I need to figure things out on my own. Sometimes, it feels easier to just shut everyone out."

"Shutting me out isn't the answer," he said, frustration creeping into his voice. "I thought we had something real, Isha. But now it feels like I'm just... invisible to you."

Her expression softened, and for a moment, he thought he saw a flicker of regret. "You're not invisible. I just... I don't know how to handle everything right now."

Abhendra's Internal Conflict

Abhendra's heart ached as he searched her face, desperate for a sign that she still cared. "I don't want to lose you. I want to be here for you, but I can't do that if you keep pushing me away."

For a brief moment, silence hung between them, thick with unspoken words. Isha bit her lip, her eyes glistening with unshed tears. "I'm scared, Abhendra. Scared of getting too close and then losing you."

The honesty in her voice cut through him. "I'm scared too. But we can face our fears together. You don't have to go through this alone."

Isha took a deep breath, and he watched as she wrestled with her emotions. "I'll try. I don't want to push you away, but it's hard to open up."

Abhendra nodded, a flicker of hope igniting within him. "That's all I ask. Just take it one step at a time. I'm not going anywhere."

As they stood there, he felt a tentative connection begin to rebuild. Isha's walls were still there, but perhaps he could help her break them down. It wouldn't be easy, but he was willing to fight for their relationship, to be the support she needed.

But as they parted ways, he couldn't shake the lingering sadness in his heart. While he felt a small glimmer of hope, the fear of being used still loomed large. Would she truly let him in, or was he destined to remain on the outside, watching her from afar?

With a heavy heart, Abhendra returned to the festivities, caught between hope and despair, wondering if this fragile connection could survive the trials that lay ahead. His internal conflict raged on, battling between the desire to be there for Isha and the haunting fear of being left behind once again.

With a heavy heart, Abhendra returned to the festivities, caught between hope and despair, wondering if this fragile connection could survive the trials that lay ahead.

"Pain is a teacher, though it doesn't always feel like one." – Abhendra Rathod

CHAPTER:5 PESSIMISTIC

The Aftermath of Their Conversation

The days that followed were a blur for Abhendra. He wrestled with his emotions, feeling both hopeful and despondent. Just when he thought he was ready to confront Isha, she remained elusive, buried under the weight of her own struggles. His mind was a whirlwind of unanswered questions, and he couldn't shake the feeling of being stuck in a cycle of uncertainty.

One evening, as he sat in his room strumming his guitar, a message notification interrupted his thoughts. It was from Isha. His heart raced as he opened it.

Isha: Hey, can we meet?

Excitement surged within him, quickly tempered by anxiety. This could be the opportunity he had been waiting for. He typed back without hesitation: *Yes! Where?*

Isha: Let's meet at our favorite café. In an hour?

As he hurried to get ready, a pit formed in his stomach. Would she finally open up? Would she confess her feelings? Or would she continue to avoid the elephant in the room? Each possibility felt like a weight pressing down on him.

When he arrived at the café, he spotted Isha sitting by the window, looking as beautiful as ever but with a hint of sadness shadowing her features. He took a deep breath and approached her table.

"Hey," he greeted, a smile on his face despite the flutter of nerves in his stomach.

"Hi," she replied, her voice soft and slightly distracted.

They sat in an awkward silence, both unsure of how to break the ice. Abhendra wanted to reach across the table, to bridge the distance between them, but the weight of their unspoken words hung heavily in the air.

"How have you been?" he finally asked, trying to keep the conversation light.

Isha shrugged, her gaze drifting outside. "It's been... complicated."

"Complicated how?" he pressed gently, sensing there was more beneath the surface.

With a sigh, she leaned back in her chair. "My grandfather is sick. The family is worried. He keeps saying he wants to see me settled before... well, before anything happens." Her voice was tinged with a mixture of sadness and frustration.

Abhendra felt a pang of sympathy for her. "I'm really sorry to hear that. Is there anything I can do to help?"

"No, it's just family stuff. They want me to get engaged soon. They think it'll make him happy," Isha admitted, her voice barely above a whisper.

Engaged? The word struck Abhendra like a physical blow. "To who?" he asked, unable to mask the concern in his voice.

"I don't know yet. They're talking to families. It all feels so sudden," she replied, her eyes clouded with uncertainty.

Abhendra's heart raced. The realization that she might be forced into a marriage sent a wave of dread through him. "But you're not dating anyone, right?"

"No, it's just… everything is happening so fast. It feels like my choices are being taken away," Isha said, her frustration evident.

"Isha, I—" Abhendra started, but she interrupted him.

"Can we not talk about that right now?" she said, her expression shifting. "I just want to focus on my family and make sure my grandfather is okay."

He felt a pang of disappointment. "Of course. But I can't help but worry about you."

"I appreciate that," she said, her gaze dropping. "But right now, it's complicated, and I don't want to drag you into my mess."

The conversation felt like a wall was being built right in front of him. "So, what does that mean for us?" he asked, desperation creeping into his voice.

"I don't know, Abhendra," she replied softly. "I just need time. I don't want to make any promises I can't keep."

"Time for what?" he pressed, feeling lost. "What do you want from me?"

"I want to figure things out with my family first. Please understand," she said, her voice trembling slightly.

Abhendra nodded, feeling the weight of her words. They were stuck in a cycle of confusion, and he was desperate to find a way out. As they left the café, a sense of hopelessness settled over him. Isha was grappling with her family's expectations, and he was left standing on the sidelines, uncertain of how to help.

Each step felt heavier than the last, the air thick with unspoken words. Pessimism crept in like a dark cloud. He couldn't shake the feeling that this would only get worse.

The thought of her getting engaged to someone else loomed large in his mind, gnawing at his confidence.

Abhendra's Feelings of Despair

What if she found happiness with someone else? What if all this time, he had been fooling himself, thinking there was something special between them? The possibility made his chest tighten with anxiety.

The distance between them felt insurmountable, and as Isha walked away, he couldn't shake the feeling that he was losing her to a future that didn't include him. He watched her retreating figure, his heart heavy with the realization that the girl he cared about was slipping away, entangled in family obligations he couldn't compete with.

Abhendra returned home that evening feeling defeated. The weight of his unexpressed feelings, combined with the harsh reality of Isha's situation, settled like a stone in his heart. The shadows of pessimism loomed larger, and he was left wondering if he would ever find a way to break free from this cycle of longing and confusion.

His guitar lay untouched in the corner of his room, a stark reminder of the music that once brought him solace.

Now, it felt like just another burden. He lay back on his bed, staring at the ceiling, grappling with the whirlwind of emotions that churned within him. Doubt seeped into every corner of his mind, filling him with despair. The future he had envisioned with Isha felt more distant than ever, overshadowed by the weight of her family's expectations.

Each passing day felt like a reminder of his helplessness. He could see Isha's smile, hear her laughter, but those moments felt like echoes of a time that was slipping away. The uncertainty gnawed at him, and he couldn't help but wonder if their connection would survive the trials that loomed ahead.

As he closed his eyes, the reality of his situation washed over him like a cold wave. He was caught in a storm of feelings, battling against the tide of pessimism that threatened to pull him under. In that moment, he realized that sometimes love wasn't enough to overcome the obstacles life threw their way.

"When the world is gray, it's hard to remember the color that once filled your heart."
–Abhendra Rathod.

CHAPTER:6 I BE FEELING PAIN

Abhendra's Coping Through Music

The days felt endless for Abhendra, each one blending into the next like a hazy dream. He had hoped that meeting Isha again would bring clarity, but instead, it deepened his confusion and pain. As the sun set each evening, he found himself drowning in a sea of unexpressed emotions, wrestling with a sense of despair that he couldn't shake.

After their last meeting, Abhendra felt as if he was caught in a storm, the winds of uncertainty howling around him. He spent hours alone in his room, strumming his guitar and pouring his heart into the music that felt like the only outlet for his anguish.

The lyrics echoed in his mind, mirroring the tumultuous feelings that twisted inside him. He could barely focus on his studies; the vibrant world around him seemed dull, overshadowed by the weight of his unreciprocated feelings for Isha.

At college, he felt like a ghost, drifting through the hallways while Isha sparkled in the company of others. Laughter and chatter surrounded him, but all he felt was isolation. He watched her from a distance, her smile lighting up the room, but it only deepened the ache in his chest.

"Abhendra, are you okay?" a friend asked one day, noticing his withdrawn demeanor.

"Yeah, I'm fine," he lied, forcing a smile. But inside, he was crumbling.

It was during a particularly dreary afternoon that Abhendra found himself sitting on a bench in the park, lost in thought. He recalled Isha's words about feeling trapped, and he wondered if she understood how much he, too, felt trapped—trapped in his own emotions and in a situation that seemed increasingly hopeless.

As he sat there, memories of their moments together flooded his mind. The way she laughed, the sparkle in her eyes when she talked about her dreams of going abroad— each memory was a bittersweet reminder of the connection he longed for but couldn't fully grasp.

Suddenly, he felt a familiar vibration in his pocket. It was a message from Isha. *I miss you. Can we talk?*

His heart raced. Maybe this was it—the chance he had been waiting for. He quickly replied, *Of course! When and where?*

Isha: How about tonight at the café?

As the evening approached, Abhendra's heart oscillated between hope and anxiety. He arrived early, pacing the café, his mind racing with possibilities. What would she say? Would she finally confess her feelings, or would she reinforce the walls that felt insurmountable?

When Isha walked in, her expression was serious, and Abhendra's heart sank slightly. "Hey," she said, sliding into the seat across from him.

"Hey," he replied, trying to read her mood.

"I've been thinking a lot," she began, her voice tinged with uncertainty. "About everything. I don't want to hurt you, but I feel so lost."

Abhendra felt a knot tighten in his stomach. "You're not hurting me. I just want to understand what's going on."

She sighed, her eyes flickering with a mix of sadness and regret. "It's just that my family is putting so much pressure on me to get engaged. I feel like I'm losing control of my life."

Abhendra's heart sank. "I know you mentioned that before. But what do you want?"

"I don't know!" she exclaimed, frustration breaking through. "I feel like I should be happy because I have so many good things going for me, but inside, I just feel... empty."

Abhendra's heart ached for her. "You don't have to make any decisions right now. Just focus on what you want."

"I wish it were that easy," she said, her voice barely above a whisper. "I'm scared, Abhendra. Scared of disappointing my family, scared of losing myself."

"You won't lose yourself. You're stronger than you think," he urged, desperate to reach her.

But as she looked away, he saw the walls begin to close in again. "You deserve someone who can give you what you need, and I can't do that right now."

His heart sank further. "Is that really how you feel?"

"I'm just being honest. I care about you, but I don't want to drag you into my mess."

"You're not dragging me into anything. I want to be here for you," he said, frustration bubbling to the surface.

"I know, but I don't want to see you get hurt," she replied, her voice trembling.

In that moment, Abhendra felt the crushing weight of despair wash over him. "I feel like I'm standing on the edge of a cliff, waiting for you to decide whether to jump or pull me down with you. It hurts, Isha."

Tears filled her eyes, and for a moment, he thought she might break down. But instead, she held herself together, her expression shifting to one of resolve. "I need time to figure things out. I hope you can understand."

As they parted that evening, the pain in his chest felt sharper than ever. He watched her walk away, her silhouette fading into the night, and the words of his lyrics replayed in his mind.

Every glance we shared felt like a spark,

But now it's silent, and I'm left in the dark.

I reached for your heart, but you looked away,

Oh Lord, take this weight, let me find my way.

The emptiness echoed around him, and he realized that this was more than just a crush; it was a deep-seated ache, a longing for something that felt just out of reach.

Reflections on Loss and Longing

In the days that followed, Abhendra made a decision. He respected Isha and her family too much to complicate her life further. If she needed space to figure things out, he would give it to her. He couldn't be the source of her stress or confusion. With a heavy heart, he blocked her number and removed her from social media, trying to sever the emotional ties that bound them.

But letting go was easier said than done. He felt an overwhelming loneliness wash over him, as if he had cut away a part of himself. The emotional pain was like a shadow that followed him everywhere, whispering reminders of the connection he had sacrificed.

Determined to channel his feelings into something productive, Abhendra immersed himself in his music. He poured his heart into writing, crafting songs that spoke of his heartache and longing. One song, *Hone Lagi*, captured the bittersweet memories of their moments together, while another, *Raat*, reflected the deep sense of loneliness that enveloped him at night.

Hone Lagi became an anthem of his feelings, expressing the joy and pain intertwined in his affection for Isha. In contrast, *Raat* painted a picture of sleepless nights filled with unanswered questions and longing. Each note, each lyric was a cathartic release, helping him navigate the emotional turmoil that consumed him.

As he performed these songs at local gigs, he found solace in the music. The crowd resonated with his pain, their applause offering a flicker of connection that eased the loneliness. Yet, even as he gained recognition, the absence of Isha left a void that no amount of applause could fill.

In the quiet moments, when the applause faded and the stage lights dimmed, the emotional scars lingered. Abhendra knew he had made the right choice for Isha, but the sacrifice weighed heavily on him. He was learning to live with the pain, finding ways to express it through art, yet the journey of healing felt long and daunting.

As the days turned into weeks, he began to realize that while he had sacrificed his connection with Isha, he was also learning to prioritize himself. The road ahead was still filled with uncertainty, but for the first time, he felt a sense of agency over his life. He was determined to rise from this heartbreak, focusing on his career and channeling his feelings into music that resonated with others, even if it meant walking a lonely path for now.

"Pain has a voice. It speaks the loudest in silence." – Abhendra Rathod

CHAPTER:7 AESTHETIC BOY

Abhendra's Rise as a Musician

As the months passed, Abhendra's journey as a musician gained momentum. He was no longer just a popular face at college; he had evolved into a public figure, admired by fans who resonated with his music and the authenticity he brought to his art. It had been a year since college ended, and the echoes of his past—particularly the memories of Isha—had begun to settle into the background, though they never truly faded.

The small café where he had his first big gig had become a regular venue for his performances. Each time he stepped onto that stage, he felt a mix of excitement and nervous energy. The audience, made up of friends, fans, and curious newcomers, filled the room with an air of anticipation. They didn't just come to hear him play; they came to experience the raw emotions he poured into his songs.

One particular evening, as the sun dipped below the horizon, casting a golden glow over the café, Abhendra prepared to share a new song. The atmosphere was charged with a sense of community—friends gathered at tables, laughter bubbling over glasses of fresh lemonade, and the warm scent of coffee wafting through the air. He adjusted his microphone and glanced out at the familiar faces before him, including Ketan, who had become a steadfast supporter of his music.

"Hey everyone! Thanks for being here tonight," Abhendra began, his voice steady but his heart racing. "I want to share a new song with you all. It's been a tough year, but I've learned a lot about love, loss, and finding myself again. This one's called *Hone Lagi*."

As he played, the chords filled the room with an emotional weight that resonated with his audience. The lyrics spoke of rediscovery, of learning to love oneself after heartbreak, and the journey of navigating complex feelings. He poured his heart into the performance, each strum echoing his growth and resilience.

After finishing, the crowd erupted into applause, their appreciation washing over him like a warm embrace. But as the evening progressed, his mind drifted back to Isha. Even in this moment of triumph, the bittersweet memory of their time together lingered.

He spotted Ketan at the bar, raising his glass in a gesture of celebration, and Abhendra felt a wave of gratitude for his friend. Ketan had always believed in him, encouraging him to embrace his artistry even during the darkest times. After the performance, Ketan joined him backstage, his expression glowing with pride.

"That was incredible, Abhendra! You've come such a long way," Ketan said, clapping him on the back. "People really connect with your music. It's like you're speaking directly to them."

"Thanks, man. It feels good to share this part of me," Abhendra replied, though a hint of uncertainty clouded his smile. "But sometimes, I still feel that emptiness. I think about Isha, you know?"

Ketan nodded, his expression softening. "It's natural to miss her. You shared something special. But remember, you're not defined by that past. You're creating a new story."

Their conversation drifted to lighter topics, but the weight of Abhendra's emotions still lingered in the back of his mind. The following week, he was scheduled to perform at a larger venue—an event that showcased emerging artists. As the date approached, he felt a mixture of excitement and anxiety. This was an opportunity to reach a broader audience, but it also meant stepping further into the spotlight.

The day of the event arrived, and the venue buzzed with energy. Abhendra felt a rush of adrenaline as he took in the vibrant crowd, each person there to experience the power of music. But as he waited for his turn, anxiety crept in. He remembered the way Isha had always encouraged him, how she had seen the potential in him even when he doubted himself. He missed her presence, her laughter, and the way she would cheer him on.

When he finally took the stage, the lights blazed down on him, and the energy in the room surged. He began with *Raat*, pouring his soul into the haunting melody. The audience fell silent, captivated by the depth of his emotion.

In the quiet of the night, I hear your name,

Whispers of a love that still feels the same.

But the stars above remind me you're far away,

And I'm left with shadows, in this endless gray.

As he sang, he felt the ache of longing but also a sense of release. Each note was a step toward healing, a way to reclaim the parts of himself that had felt lost. When the final chord resonated, the audience erupted in applause, their appreciation washing over him like a wave.

After the performance, he was greeted by fans eager to connect. They shared their own stories of heartbreak and resilience, and for the first time in a while, Abhendra felt a genuine sense of belonging. Yet, amidst the cheers and admiration, the memory of Isha remained a bittersweet undertone, an unresolved chapter in his heart.

Moments of Success Overshadowed by Memories

In the following days, Abhendra received messages from fans who had been touched by his music. One message caught his eye—a young girl named Neha expressed how *Raat* had resonated with her own experiences of love and loss. Her words stirred something within him, and he felt a renewed sense of purpose. Maybe his music could help others find their way through their pain, just as it had helped him.

But even as he found joy in his work, the absence of Isha loomed large. One evening, while scrolling through social media, he stumbled upon a photo of her with someone else—a smiling face, an arm draped casually around her shoulders. The image hit him like a punch to the gut, igniting a mix of jealousy and sorrow. He quickly looked away, heart racing, reminding himself of his choice to prioritize her happiness.

In the weeks that followed, Abhendra immersed himself in his music and collaborations. He wrote feverishly, drawing inspiration from the complexities of life and love. But each time he strummed the guitar or jotted down lyrics, he felt the familiar pang of longing and loss creep back in.

During one of his late-night writing sessions, he found himself questioning his choices. He had let Isha go for her own sake, yet why did it still feel like such a heavy burden? Was it selfish to want her in his life, even as he respected her family's wishes?

It was during a conversation with Ketan that the truth began to crystallize. They met at their favorite park, surrounded by the vibrant colors of autumn leaves. As they sat on a bench, sipping their drinks, Ketan looked at him with a knowing expression.

"You can't keep carrying this weight, Abhendra. You made a choice, and it was a brave one, but it doesn't mean you can't also seek happiness for yourself. Have you thought about what you really want?"

Abhendra paused, letting Ketan's words sink in. "I want to create. I want to connect with people through my music. But I also don't want to hurt her, you know? I don't want to be the reason she feels trapped or obligated."

"Then maybe it's time to reach out," Ketan suggested gently. "Not to disrupt her life, but to find closure for yourself. You deserve that too."

As the sun dipped below the horizon, casting long shadows across the park, Abhendra felt a shift within him. Maybe it was time to confront the lingering emotions that had held him captive for so long. Maybe it was time to let go of the fear and embrace the possibility of connection once more.

That night, as he returned home, Abhendra picked up his guitar and began to play a new melody. The chords flowed effortlessly, merging with the emotions he had been grappling with. He wrote about the beauty of love, the pain of separation, and the hope for healing. The song emerged as a tribute to his journey—a testament to the strength found in vulnerability.

He titled it *Aesthetic Boy*, a reflection of the multifaceted nature of his experiences. In the lyrics, he embraced his journey as an artist and a person, acknowledging the moments of darkness but celebrating the light that had emerged from them.

As he finished writing, he felt a sense of relief wash over him. The song was more than just music; it was a declaration of his growth, a reminder that while pain was a part of life, so was the potential for joy. With each note, he felt like he was carving a new path, one that honored his past but didn't allow it to define him.

In the days that followed, Abhendra took the leap. He drafted a message to Isha, hesitating for a moment before pressing send. He knew that reaching out could open old wounds, but he also understood the importance of closure—for both of them.

Hey Isha, it's been a while. I hope you're doing well. I've been thinking about our time together and wanted to reconnect, just to see how you are. No pressure. Just wanted to reach out.

After sending the message, he felt a mix of anxiety and hope. He had taken the first step toward confronting the unresolved feelings that lingered. Whatever response he received, he knew he had to allow himself the chance to find closure.

In the weeks that followed, Abhendra continued to perform, sharing his new songs with the world. But beneath the surface, he waited, holding onto a flicker of hope that Isha would respond. Life continued to unfold—beautifully chaotic and unpredictably real. Each day

became an opportunity to create, to connect, and to grow. And as he stepped further into his journey, he understood that he was not just an aesthetic boy; he was a storyteller, weaving the tapestry of his life through music and art.

The moment of reckoning was coming, and he was ready to face whatever lay ahead.

> **"Sometimes, the most beautiful things are hidden in the brokenness of a soul."**
>
> **–Abhendra Rathod**

CHAPTER:8 DESPAIR

The News of Isha's Impending Wedding

The months that followed Abhendra's message to Isha had been transformative. His music career blossomed in ways he had only dreamed of—gigs at packed venues, collaborations with talented artists, and a growing fan base that celebrated the raw authenticity of his work. He was no longer just a face in the crowd; he had become a voice, a storyteller whose lyrics resonated with many. Each performance was a cathartic release, a way to channel his emotions into something beautiful, and the applause he received felt like a warm embrace.

Yet, beneath the veneer of success, a hollowness lingered. He was caught in a whirlwind of triumph and heartache, feeling the pangs of unfulfilled love echoing through the spaces he tried to fill with music. The thrill of the spotlight was bittersweet; no matter how many fans sang along to his lyrics, he felt an emptiness that would not dissipate.

Every time he took the stage, he would look out into the audience and scan for familiar faces—friends, supporters, people who had been there through his journey. But as he searched, he always found himself wishing to see Isha there, her smile lighting up the room. He had spent so much time convincing himself that letting her go was the right thing, yet each day brought a fresh reminder of the connection they once shared. He found himself grappling with questions that had no answers, like a song stuck on repeat in his mind.

One evening, while he was winding down after a particularly electrifying performance, he received a notification on his phone. It was a post from a mutual friend—a photo that turned his world upside down.

"Congratulations, Isha! Excited to celebrate your wedding!"

The words were simple, yet they struck him like lightning. The accompanying image showed Isha in a stunning traditional outfit, beaming with happiness, surrounded by friends and family. In that moment, the air around him felt thick and suffocating. He felt as if the ground had been pulled out from under him, leaving him teetering on the edge of a precipice.

A wave of emotions crashed over him—shock, despair, and a sense of overwhelming regret. It was as if the world had gone still, and he was the only one left in motion, spiraling into a dark abyss. He had spent months believing he was doing the right thing by letting her go, yet in that moment, he realized the profound depth of his feelings for her.

He had always known they shared something special, a bond that transcended the ordinary. Yet he had convinced himself that stepping back was an act of love, a way to ensure she found her happiness without the complications of his own emotions. Now, that choice felt like a cruel joke, a betrayal to both of their hearts.

The days that followed felt like an endless cycle of grief. He went through the motions of his life, performing at gigs, engaging with fans, and creating music, but his heart was heavy with a sorrow that refused to lift. The laughter and applause that once filled him with joy now rang hollow in his ears. Each time he played a song that reminded him of Isha, he felt the weight of longing settle deeper in his chest.

As he scrolled through social media, the images of Isha's wedding continued to flood his feed. Photos of her with friends, laughing, dancing, and looking radiant, tore at his heart. He felt an urge to reach out, to find some way to reconnect, but the fear of disrupting her life kept him paralyzed. Would she even want to hear from him? Had he been reduced to a fleeting memory in her life, someone she had loved but had moved on from?

He couldn't escape the gnawing realization that he had made a choice—a choice that now felt like a prison. He had let her go, believing it was for the best, but now he felt trapped in his own regret. The thought of Isha embarking on a new journey without him felt unbearable. Would she be happy? Did she truly want this? Or was she simply fulfilling the expectations placed upon her by her family?

Abhendra's Realization of His Feelings

One evening, unable to cope with the turmoil inside him, Abhendra picked up his guitar and started strumming absentmindedly. The chords felt foreign, as if they were mocking him. The melodies he once found solace in escaped him. He tried to write a new song, something to articulate the chaos in his heart, but nothing seemed to come.

I let you go, thinking it was right,

But now I'm left here, lost in the night.

You're moving on, while I stand still,

Crushed by the weight of unspoken will.

With every strum, the heaviness in his chest deepened. Abhendra's thoughts turned to Isha and the countless moments they had shared—the laughter, the dreams, the unspoken connection that had always lingered between them. He thought of how she must have felt, trapped by the expectations of her family while he stood by, paralyzed, thinking he was doing the right thing.

Did she ever question his decision? Did she wonder why he hadn't fought for them, for their love? The thought pierced him like a dagger, leaving him breathless. He remembered their late-night talks, her eyes sparkling with dreams and aspirations, and how they had imagined a future together, one filled with music and adventure. Now, it felt like a cruel mirage, fading further into the distance.

In a fit of frustration, Abhendra put the guitar down and grabbed his phone, contemplating whether to reach out to Isha again. But fear gripped him, holding him back like a vice. What if she had truly moved on? What if he was just another fleeting memory in her life? He felt torn between the desire to reconnect and the fear of rejection. The emotional conflict left him drained, spiraling deeper into despair.

Ketan, his loyal friend, noticed the change in Abhendra. One night, they met at their favorite bar, the lively atmosphere clashing with the heaviness that hung over Abhendra. Ketan studied him, his expression shifting from concern to determination.

"You need to talk about this, Abhendra. You've been so distant lately," Ketan said, setting his drink down with a decisive thud.

Abhendra sighed, feeling the weight of Ketan's words. "It's Isha. She's getting married, and I can't shake the feeling that I let her slip away. I thought I was doing the right thing, but now... it feels like a mistake."

Ketan's brow furrowed. "You did what you thought was right. But it's okay to feel this way. You loved her, and now you're grieving. It's a heavy burden."

"I keep thinking about all the moments we shared," Abhendra admitted, his voice cracking. "The way she looked at me when I played, how she believed in me when I doubted myself. And now she's moving on. I feel so lost."

Ketan leaned in closer, his expression softening. "But what do you want? What's stopping you from reaching out to her?"

Abhendra ran a hand through his hair, frustration boiling over. "I want to know how she is. I want to tell her that I still care. But what if she's happy? What if she doesn't want to hear from me?"

"Then you'll never know," Ketan replied gently. "You can't keep carrying this weight, Abhendra. You made a choice, and it was a brave one, but it doesn't mean you can't also seek happiness for yourself. You deserve that too."

As the sun dipped below the horizon, casting long shadows across the bar, Abhendra felt a shift within him. Maybe it was time to confront the lingering emotions that had held him captive for so long. Maybe it was time to let go of the fear and embrace the possibility of connection once more.

That night, as he returned home, Abhendra picked up his guitar and began to play a new melody. The chords flowed effortlessly, merging with the emotions he had been grappling with. He wrote about the beauty of love, the pain of separation, and the hope for healing. The song emerged as a tribute to his journey—a testament to the strength found in vulnerability.

He titled it *Aesthetic Boy*, a reflection of the multifaceted nature of his experiences. In the lyrics, he embraced his journey as an artist and a person, acknowledging the moments of darkness but celebrating the light that had emerged from them.

As he finished writing, he felt a sense of relief wash over him. The song was more than just music; it was a declaration of his growth, a reminder that while pain was a part of life, so was the potential for joy. With each note, he felt like he was carving a new path, one that honored his past but didn't allow it to define him.

But even as he crafted this new anthem of self-discovery, the shadow of Isha's impending wedding loomed large. The thought of her starting a new life with someone else gnawed at him relentlessly. He tried to push it away, to focus on the music and the community that had embraced him, but it felt like trying to hold water in his hands—it slipped through his fingers no matter how hard he tried.

Days turned into weeks, and Abhendra continued to perform, sharing his new songs with the world. But beneath the surface, he waited, holding onto a flicker of hope that Isha would respond to his previous message. Each day felt like an eternity, a mix of anticipation and dread.

Finally, after what felt like ages, he received a notification that made his heart

race—an unread message from Isha. He stared at the screen, his hands trembling. Should he open it? Should he let himself hope? Taking a deep breath, he clicked on the message.

"Hey Abhendra, it's great to hear from you! I hope you've been well. I've been thinking about our time together, too. Let's catch up soon?"

The words washed over him like a wave, stirring a complex mix of joy and anxiety. They hadn't lost the connection he had feared would fade away completely. But before he could formulate a response, the reality of her impending wedding crashed into him like a tidal wave. What did she want to talk about? Was this just a friendly check-in, or was there something deeper lingering beneath the surface?

He spent the night wrestling with his thoughts, his mind racing as he tried to weigh his options. Should he confess his feelings, risking everything? Or should he keep it light and friendly, preserving the fragile connection they had? The fear of losing her again gripped him tightly.

As the wedding day approached, Abhendra felt the weight of his emotions pressing down on him. He decided to respond, crafting a message that balanced his feelings with a desire to respect her new path.

"Hey Isha! It's so good to hear from you. I'd love to catch up. Just let me know when you're free!"

The reply came almost instantly.

"Let's meet this weekend? I'd love to see you!"

With that simple exchange, a flicker of hope ignited within him. But along with it came a rush of anxiety. What would he say? Would they be able to talk freely, or would the shadows of their past loom over them? He could already envision Isha, radiant and happy, dressed in white, standing with someone else, and the thought tore at his heart.

On the day of their meeting, Abhendra arrived at the café they used to frequent, his nerves dancing wildly in his stomach. He took a seat at a table in the corner, the familiar ambiance filling him with nostalgia. The café was a backdrop to so many memories—late-night talks, laughter, and the warmth of their shared dreams. But today, it felt different, heavy with unspoken words and lingering feelings.

When Isha walked in, time seemed to stand still. She looked beautiful, her eyes sparkling with life, and yet he could see the slight tension in her posture. They exchanged smiles, and Abhendra felt a rush of memories flood back—moments of connection that had once defined them.

"Hey! It's so good to see you," she said, her voice warm but tinged with something unnameable.

"You too. You look amazing," he replied, feeling a knot tighten in his chest. "Congratulations on the wedding."

"Thank you," she said, her smile faltering for a moment. "It's been… a lot, you know?"

Abhendra nodded, the weight of their shared past hanging between them like a thread waiting to snap. "I can only imagine. I've been… working on my music. Trying to find my way."

"I've seen some of your performances online. You've come so far," she said, genuine admiration in her eyes.

They settled into the conversation, but it felt like navigating a minefield. Each question seemed laden with unspoken implications, each answer pulled them closer yet kept them apart. They talked about their lives, their passions, and the dreams they once shared. But the elephant in the room—his feelings for her, the way their paths had diverged—loomed large.

"Do you ever think about us?" he finally blurted out, the words spilling from his lips before he could stop them.

Isha's expression shifted, surprise flickering in her eyes. "All the time," she admitted softly, looking down at her coffee. "I've wondered why you didn't fight for us, why you let me go."

Abhendra felt his heart race, the truth of his feelings hanging in the air between them. "I thought it was for the best. I wanted you to be happy, even if it meant being apart."

"But what about your happiness?" she asked, her voice tinged with frustration. "Did you ever consider what I wanted? I never wanted to lose you."

The words struck him like a bolt of lightning, illuminating the dark corners of his despair. He opened his mouth to speak but found himself at a loss for words. Instead, he reached out and took her hand, their fingers intertwining—a connection that felt both familiar and electrifying.

"I thought letting you go was the right choice, but now... I see how wrong I was. I miss you, Isha. I've never stopped loving you."

Tears shimmered in her eyes as she met his gaze. "I've thought about you too. So many times, I wondered what could have been. But now... I'm about to start a new chapter, and I don't know how to reconcile that with what we had."

Abhendra's heart sank as he realized the gravity of their situation. The weight of unfulfilled dreams hung heavy in the air. "I never wanted to hold you back," he confessed, feeling vulnerable for the first time. "But I also can't ignore how I feel."

They sat in silence, the café bustling around them, but it felt as if time had stopped. Each heartbeat echoed the truth they had danced around for so long. Isha looked down, her expression clouded with conflicting emotions.

"I have to think about my family, my future," she said softly, almost as if she were trying to convince herself. "But a part of me has always wanted to be with you. It's just... complicated."

"Life is complicated," Abhendra replied, his voice steadier than he felt. "But that doesn't mean we should ignore what we feel."

The weight of his words hung in the air, and Isha's expression shifted, a flicker of hope crossing her face. "What if I choose this path? What does that mean for us?"

Abhendra squeezed her hand gently. "It means we need to be honest with ourselves. If you're happy, I want that for you. But if there's still a chance for us, I don't want to walk away without knowing."

They left the café that day with more questions than answers, but for the first time in a long time, Abhendra felt a glimmer of hope. It was a small step, but it was a step toward understanding—toward healing the wounds that had festered for so long.

As he walked home, he couldn't shake the feeling that their paths were intertwined in ways that transcended the boundaries of time and circumstance. He had taken a leap of faith, and though he was still grappling with despair, he realized that love, in all its complexity, was worth fighting for.

In the days that followed, Abhendra poured his heart into his music, channeling the emotions of that meeting into new songs. He felt an urgency to express everything he had bottled up inside—his love, his pain, and his hope for the future. Each note became a cathartic release, a way to process the tumultuous feelings swirling within him.

But as the wedding date drew closer, he couldn't help but feel the weight of despair creeping back in. Isha was embarking on a journey that he could only watch from the sidelines, and despite their connection, he still felt an overwhelming sense of loss.

In the end, he knew he had to confront the reality of their situation. They were both at a crossroads, and whatever path they chose would shape their lives in ways they could not yet comprehend.

And as he continued to pour himself into his music, he understood that while despair was a part of the journey, it was not the end of the road. There was still hope—hope that love could transcend time and distance, that their paths could converge once more.

Abhendra was determined to honor the complexity of their emotions, to embrace the uncertainty that lay ahead. For in the depths of despair, he also found the seeds of resilience, and with each note he played, he reclaimed a piece of himself.

He was not just an aesthetic boy; he was a storyteller, navigating the intricacies of life and love, ready to face whatever lay ahead.

"Despair doesn't mean the end; it means the soul is aching for change." – Abhendra Rathod

CHAPTER:9 BROKEN

Isha's Marriage and Abhendra's Isolation

The day of Isha's wedding dawned bright and clear, yet Abhendra felt an oppressive darkness settle over him. He had dreaded this day, knowing deep down it marked the finality of something beautiful and fragile. For months, he had steeled himself against the memories of her laughter and their shared dreams, but now, as he stood before the mirror, the weight of his choices pressed heavily on his chest.

He slipped into a formal suit, a garment that felt suffocating, a stark reminder of the occasion he was not invited to but felt compelled to witness. The red and gold decorations he glimpsed through the window hinted at the grandeur of Indian weddings, a celebration he had once hoped would include him at Isha's side. But today, he was merely a shadow, lurking on the fringes of a life that had moved on without him.

As he arrived at the venue, the sight of the lavish decorations struck him. The hall was adorned with vibrant flowers, twinkling fairy lights, and rich fabrics that swayed gently in the afternoon breeze. Laughter and music floated through the air, creating a festive atmosphere that felt worlds apart from the turmoil raging inside him.

In the back of the hall, he lingered, scanning the crowd for a glimpse of her. And then, like a burst of sunlight cutting through the clouds, he spotted Isha. She was a vision in a stunning red lehenga, her face aglow with happiness. The intricate embroidery of her outfit sparkled as she moved, and he felt his heart clench painfully in his chest. She looked breathtaking, yet it was a beauty that felt like a dagger piercing his soul.

As the ceremony began, Abhendra's world narrowed down to Isha and the man standing beside her, a stranger who now claimed a piece of her heart. The priest's chants filled the air, but Abhendra was deaf to the words. Each vow exchanged felt like a chisel chipping away at his spirit. He wanted to scream, to run forward and take her hand, to remind her of all the moments they had shared—the laughter, the dreams, the love that had once flowed so freely between them. But he remained rooted to the spot, a statue of regret.

He noticed a few familiar faces in the crowd, friends from college, but they offered him no solace. They were there to celebrate a love he felt he had lost, and not one of them approached him. It stung, a sharp reminder of his self-imposed exile. He felt invisible, as if he were a ghost haunting the edges of a life that no longer included him.

As the couple exchanged garlands and tied the sacred knot, Abhendra's heart shattered into a million pieces. The realization struck him with brutal clarity: he had let her go, and in doing so, he had lost the most important part of himself. He had made the choice to prioritize her happiness over his own, believing it was the right thing to do, but now, watching her marry someone else, he questioned every decision he had made.

With each passing moment, he felt a deeper sense of despair wash over him. He was overwhelmed by the bitter taste of regret. *Why hadn't he fought for her?* The question echoed in his mind, a relentless reminder of his cowardice. As the ceremony continued, Abhendra found himself slipping away from the crowd, unable to bear the sight of her happiness.

He wandered into the beautifully landscaped garden, where the bright colors of flowers contrasted sharply with his desolation. The laughter and joy of the celebration faded into the background, replaced by the deafening silence of his thoughts. He could still hear the vows, the promises of love and loyalty that sealed Isha's fate with someone else.

Sitting on a bench under a tree, he felt the weight of his choices crash over him like a wave. It was as if the universe had conspired against him, mocking him for his indecision. *You let her go,* the voice in his head taunted. *Now you must live with the consequences.*

Days turned into weeks, and the pain of her wedding lingered like an open wound. Abhendra retreated further into himself, isolating in the four walls of his room. The guitar he had once poured his soul into now lay silent in the corner, a relic of a happier time. Music had been his escape, his outlet, but now it felt like a cruel reminder of all that he had lost.

Transition to a New Job in a Medical College

The world outside continued to spin, but inside his bubble of despair, time stood still. He immersed himself in work, applying for a position as a lab technician at a local medical college. Science had always fascinated him, and he hoped that a new environment might help distract him from the storm of emotions raging within.

When he finally received the job offer, it felt like a lifeline. He threw himself into his work, learning the ins and outs of laboratory procedures and techniques. The sterile environment of the lab provided a refuge, a place where he could focus on tasks that required his full attention. Each day was filled with the routine of testing samples, analyzing results, and preparing reports, providing a sense of purpose he had been desperately craving.

But just as he began to find his footing, the world was struck by the COVID-19 pandemic. Lockdowns, social distancing, and the chaos that ensued shifted the dynamics of his new job. Abhendra was thrust onto the front lines, assisting in testing and research efforts. The urgency of the situation distracted him from his internal struggles, and for the first time in a long while, he felt a sense of responsibility that overshadowed his grief.

As patients flooded into the medical facility, Abhendra witnessed the strength and resilience of those facing unimaginable challenges. The fear and uncertainty in their eyes mirrored his own, yet their courage inspired him. He channeled his energy into helping others, finding solace in the act of service. In the chaos of the pandemic, he learned to appreciate the fragility of life and the importance of connection.

The months dragged on, marked by long hours and sleepless nights. Each day, he faced the reality of loss—both in terms of loved ones to the virus and in his own heart. But amidst the sorrow, there was also hope. Abhendra began to see glimpses of light, moments of kindness and solidarity that reminded him of the beauty still present in the world.

Yet, even as he dedicated himself to his work, the shadows of his past loomed large. Late at night, when he returned home to the silence of his room, memories of Isha invaded his thoughts. He often wondered how she was, what her new life was like, and whether she ever thought of him. The longing for her companionship gnawed at him, but he pushed those feelings deep down, afraid to confront them.

Weeks turned into months, and Abhendra's routine settled into a pattern that provided some semblance of stability. He volunteered for community testing events, immersing himself in the work, trying to forget the emptiness that lingered within. But as the world slowly began to reopen, he felt an internal conflict. The routine that had once shielded him from pain now felt like a cage, trapping him in a cycle of neutrality devoid of passion.

One quiet evening, after a particularly long day, Abhendra picked up his guitar for the first time in ages. He sat on the edge of his bed, fingers hovering over the strings, and took a deep breath. As he began to play, the familiar chords washed over him, stirring emotions he had tried to suppress. It was a bittersweet melody that echoed his heartache, a song of love and loss.

As he played, tears streamed down his face, each note a reminder of the joy Isha had brought into his life. The music became a release, a way to acknowledge the pain he had tried to hide. He played for Isha, for the memories they had created together, and for the love that would forever remain a part of him.

In that moment of vulnerability, Abhendra accepted his brokenness. He understood that it was okay to feel pain, to mourn the loss of what could have been. He was not defined solely by his past but by how he chose to move forward.

With renewed determination, he decided to integrate music back into his life—not as an escape, but as a form of expression. He began writing again, channeling his experiences into songs that reflected his journey. Each lyric became a testament to his resilience, a way to honor the love he had lost while also celebrating the person he was becoming.

Abhendra may have been broken, but he was learning to rebuild, piece by piece, note by note. And while the road ahead was uncertain, he finally felt ready to embrace it—full of hope, healing, and the possibility of new beginnings.

"To be broken is not a curse, but a chance to rebuild something stronger."—Abhendra Rathod

CHAPTER:10 NO MORE LOVE

Abhendra's Transformation and Growth

The months after Isha's wedding felt like a heavy fog hanging over Abhendra. While he tried to move on with his life, he often found himself lost in thoughts of her, the memories of their shared laughter and dreams drifting through his mind like ghosts. Every morning, he woke up feeling the weight of a world that had shifted overnight, leaving him with an empty space where love once flourished.

Abhendra threw himself into his work as a lab technician, immersing himself in the demands of the medical field. Days turned into nights filled with tests, samples, and the relentless rhythm of life at the college. It kept him busy, kept his mind occupied, but the moments of quiet still struck him like a lightning bolt, jolting him back to memories of Isha. He could almost hear her laughter echoing in his mind, and the ache in his heart would flare up again.

"Hey, Abhendra! You killed it in the lab today!" his colleague Priya said one afternoon, breaking through his reverie.

"Thanks, Priya," he replied, offering a half-hearted smile. He appreciated her enthusiasm but felt nothing beneath the surface. His heart was still wrapped in layers of hurt, unable to fully engage with the world around him.

Life continued its relentless march. Abhendra had become well-known for his music, performing at local cafes and events. Fans approached him after shows, excited to share how his songs had touched their lives. But each time someone praised his work, he felt a bittersweet pang—recognition felt hollow when he was wrestling with his own emotions.

One night, after a performance, a group of young women approached him, their eyes sparkling with admiration. "You were amazing! We love your music!" one of them exclaimed, her excitement palpable.

"Thanks, I really appreciate it," he said, his voice distant. He smiled politely, but inside, he felt an emptiness that couldn't be filled by compliments or attention. The warmth of their interest felt like a flicker of light in a dark room—temporary, fleeting.

In the months that followed, Abhendra began to erect walls around his heart. He made a vow to himself: *No more love.* Love had brought him joy, but it had also brought him pain—pain that felt too heavy to bear again. He started to avoid situations where he might connect with others on a deeper level. The thought of risking his heart made him uneasy, and he retreated into a world of solitude.

As he immersed himself in work and music, he began to notice a shift in his personality. The vibrant, carefree artist had transformed into a more serious, guarded individual. He became someone who felt more like a shell of his former self—still talented, still capable, but no longer able to embrace the joy he once found in life.

Friends tried to coax him out of his shell. Ketan, always the optimistic one, would often nudge him. "You can't let one heartbreak define you, Abhendra! There are so many amazing people out there just waiting to get to know you!"

But Abhendra would just shake his head. "I'm fine. Really. I just want to focus on my music and work. That's enough for me." Deep down, he knew he was lying, but it felt safer to pretend.

One evening, as he sat in his dimly lit room, strumming his guitar softly, he felt a surge of emotions. He poured his heart into his music, crafting songs that resonated with his struggles. He wrote about love and loss, but even as he did, he felt the weight of his decision to close himself off. It was cathartic, but it also felt like a band-aid over a deep wound that refused to heal.

He penned a song he titled *No More Love,* capturing his resolve to move on. Each lyric was a reflection of the emotional armor he had constructed around his heart:

No more love, I close my door,

The echoes of your laughter, I can't take anymore.

I've built these walls, strong and tall,

To keep the heartache from making me fall.

As he sang those words, he felt a bittersweet release. He had turned his pain into something tangible, yet he also recognized that he was burying a part of himself in the process. Love, for all its heartache, had also been a source of joy and connection. He was denying himself the chance to experience those feelings again.

The months passed, and the pain of Isha's absence began to feel like a dull ache. He had built a routine around work and music, but it was a routine steeped in solitude. He noticed how people admired him for his talent, but the adoration felt superficial compared to the depth of love he once shared.

Then one day, as he was scrolling through social media during his lunch break, he stumbled upon a post that stopped him cold. A photograph of Isha, radiant and happy, appeared on his screen. She was surrounded by friends, her smile brighter than he remembered, and the caption read: *"So grateful to be marrying the love of my life today!"*

The world tilted beneath him. Abhendra felt as if he had been punched in the gut. The weight of realization crashed over him—he had let her go. He had been so focused on protecting himself that he hadn't fought for her, for the love they shared.

His heart raced, and his palms grew clammy as he read the comments filled with congratulations and excitement. He was happy for her, truly, but a part of him felt like it was burning away. Memories flooded back—moments they had shared, dreams they had discussed, and the deep connection they had built.

Why didn't I do anything? he thought. *Why didn't I fight for us?*

His mind raced with questions. Isha had always believed in him, had always been there to support him. But when it came to love, he had retreated, thinking it was the noble choice, the right thing to do. He had respected her family's wishes, but now, it felt like the biggest mistake of his life.

He felt the tears welling up in his eyes, a mix of anger and sorrow. Abhendra quickly closed his laptop, feeling suffocated by the reality of the moment. He wanted to scream, to lash out at the world for the unfairness of it all. Instead, he sat in silence, grappling with the emotional storm raging inside him.

Rejecting New Relationships

The weeks that followed were unbearable. Abhendra found himself withdrawing further into isolation. The vibrant life he had once embraced faded into a dull routine of work and the occasional performance. He spent countless evenings locked in his room, strumming his guitar but unable to find the energy or inspiration to create.

He had lost something vital, and now he was left feeling broken. It was a darkness that clung to him, one he couldn't shake off. While he had promised himself *no more love*, he found that the absence of love left an even larger void.

It was during one of those long, quiet nights that he realized he needed to take action. He had to face the truth about his feelings, about what he had lost, and the life he had chosen. He started to seek out new opportunities, feeling a desperate need to engage with the world again.

As luck would have it, a position opened up in the local hospital's laboratory. The role involved working closely with medical professionals during the COVID-19 pandemic, supporting testing and research efforts. The idea of helping others resonated with him, and he decided to apply.

When he received the job offer, a small flicker of hope ignited within him. This was a chance to channel his energy into something meaningful, to support those in need during such a trying time. He began his new role with determination, immersing himself in the work and dedicating his skills to the fight against the virus.

Each day brought new challenges, but with them came a renewed sense of purpose. He felt like he was making a difference, helping people at their most vulnerable. In the chaos of the hospital, he found moments of connection with colleagues who were just as passionate about making a difference.

Yet, even in this new environment, Abhendra still felt the weight of his heartache. He took breaks to sit in quiet corners, allowing himself to process his feelings in solitude. He began to understand that while he could bury his emotions, they wouldn't disappear.

As the pandemic wore on, Abhendra found himself gradually moving through the stages of grief he had avoided for so long. He acknowledged the pain of his loss, allowing himself to feel it without judgment. He wrote in his journal, capturing his thoughts about love, heartbreak, and the complexity of human emotions.

Through it all, he kept his guitar close. He took breaks to play, pouring his feelings into his music once more. Although he had stepped back from performing publicly, he felt the urge to create again, to channel his experiences into songs that resonated with the struggles of others.

The pain of losing Isha was still there, but he began to understand it differently. He realized that love, even when it leads to heartbreak, shapes who we are. It teaches us lessons about ourselves and our capacity for connection.

As he started to heal, he felt more open to the idea of love again, though cautiously. He didn't want to rush into anything, but the thought of possibly reconnecting with someone, of allowing himself to feel again, began to take root in his mind.

With the passing months, Abhendra gradually started to re-engage with the music scene. His friends encouraged him to perform again, reminding him of how much joy he brought to others. While part of him was still hesitant, he felt a

growing desire to share his story, to connect with people through the art he loved.

As he prepared for his first performance back, he reflected on his journey—the pain, the despair, and the eventual realization that life is too precious to shut oneself off completely. He had learned that love could be both a source of joy and pain, but it was also a pathway to growth.

He stepped onto the stage, feeling the familiar rush of adrenaline course through him. The crowd erupted into applause, and as he took a deep breath, he felt a sense of belonging. He was ready to embrace the complexities of love and life again.

With each song, he shared not only his journey but also the message that while love can lead us into darkness, it can also guide us back into the light.

As Abhendra sang, he knew he wasn't just performing; he was reclaiming a part of himself. The music flowed through him, and he felt a sense of liberation. It was a new chapter, one where love would be a part of his life, but not the only part.

And in that moment, he understood that he was not broken—he was simply evolving, learning to love himself and the world around him again.

"When love has left, what remains is the echo of what was once everything."

– Abhendra Rathod

CHAPTER:11 WHO AM I ?

A Journey of Self-Discovery

As Abhendra stepped off the stage after his performance, the applause still ringing in his ears, he felt a rush of emotions that he hadn't experienced in a long time. The thrill of sharing his music with an audience, the warmth of their appreciation—it all felt like a distant memory that had suddenly returned to life. Yet, amidst the excitement, a deeper question lingered at the back of his mind: *Who am I?*

It was a question he had been grappling with since Isha's wedding. After years of defining himself through his relationships and passions, he now found himself at a crossroads, trying to piece together a new identity. He had built walls around his heart, declaring *no more love,* yet here he was, standing in front of a crowd, a musician once again. But was he still the same Abhendra he had been before heartbreak had shadowed his life?

In the weeks following his comeback performance, he became increasingly reflective. The music industry buzzed with energy, filled with the excitement of new projects and collaborations. Abhendra was invited to events, parties, and gatherings where fellow musicians mingled and exchanged ideas. Yet, each time he stepped into a new social setting, he felt like an outsider looking in.

"Abhendra, you're back! It's so great to see you performing again!" one of his peers exclaimed at a music launch party.

"Thanks! It feels good to be back," he replied, forcing a smile. But inside, he was questioning whether he truly belonged to this vibrant world anymore.

He found himself watching others interact, noting their ease in social situations, their laughter and camaraderie. They moved through conversations like dancers, while he felt like a wallflower, unsure of his next step. *Who am I in this space?* he wondered. Was he just a name people recognized, or was there more to him than that?

Days turned into weeks, and as he navigated this new reality, the question loomed larger. He sought solace in his music, pouring his feelings into lyrics, attempting to explore his identity through his art. He wrote song after song, each one delving deeper into his psyche, asking questions he hadn't dared to voice aloud:

Who am I without you?

Just a ghost in the crowd, searching for clues.

Was I the dreamer, or just a fool?

In a world of noise, I'm losing my cool.

As he played these new songs, he found a cathartic release. Each note became a stepping stone toward understanding himself anew. He reflected on his past—his dreams, his fears, and his relationship with Isha. It was a complex tapestry woven with moments of joy and pain, love and loss.

One evening, after a particularly introspective writing session, he decided to reach out to Ketan. They met at their favorite café, where the aroma of freshly brewed coffee mingled with the chatter of patrons. As they settled into their seats, Abhendra felt a familiar comfort wash over him.

"Hey, man. It's good to see you," Ketan said, genuine warmth in his voice.

"Good to be here. I've been thinking a lot lately," Abhendra admitted, stirring his coffee absently.

Ketan raised an eyebrow, his interest piqued. "About what?"

"About who I am. I feel like I've changed so much, but I can't quite grasp who I've become," Abhendra confessed.

Ketan leaned forward, encouraging him to continue. "It's natural to feel that way after everything you've been through. Change is a part of life. What's making you question yourself?"

"I guess it's this feeling of being lost," Abhendra replied, running a hand through his hair. "I used to be so certain of who I was—an artist, a musician, someone in love. Now, I feel like I'm just... floating."

Ketan nodded thoughtfully. "It's okay to float for a while. Sometimes we need that space to explore different sides of ourselves. Have you considered what you want beyond music?"

Abhendra paused, contemplating Ketan's question. "I've been so focused on my music and healing that I haven't thought about much else. But maybe... maybe I want to explore new things, see who I can be outside of the spotlight."

"That sounds like a great idea," Ketan encouraged. "You're not just a musician; you're a person with interests, passions, and dreams. Why not explore them?"

As the conversation continued, Abhendra felt a shift within himself. Ketan's perspective opened a door he hadn't realized was there. The idea of redefining himself, of exploring new avenues, excited him. It was an opportunity to answer the question of who he was in a broader context.

In the days that followed, he began to seek out new experiences. He attended workshops on photography, a hobby he had always wanted to explore but never had the time for. He signed up for cooking classes, discovering a joy in creating dishes that reminded him of home. Each new experience peeled back layers of his identity, revealing facets he had long forgotten.

Yet, even as he dived into these new activities, Abhendra often found himself reflecting on his relationship with Isha. He wondered how she was doing, if she thought about him, and if she too was exploring her identity in this new chapter of her life. It was a complicated mix of emotions, and he learned to hold space for those feelings without letting them consume him.

One afternoon, while sitting on the beach with his camera, capturing the golden hues of sunset, Abhendra felt a wave of clarity wash over him. He realized that his identity was not confined to a single label—musician, artist, lover—but was instead a mosaic of experiences, emotions, and connections.

He was an artist, yes, but he was also a friend, a dreamer, a seeker of beauty in the mundane. With each snapshot he took, he embraced the fullness of his existence, recognizing that the journey of self-discovery was ongoing.

Questioning Identity and Purpose

It was during this period of exploration that he decided to return to music, but on his own terms. He envisioned an album that encapsulated his journey over the past year—the heartbreak, the healing, and the rediscovery of self. He wanted to share not just his pain but also the lessons he had learned about love, resilience, and identity.

In the studio, as he poured his heart into new melodies, he felt invigorated. This time, the songs flowed freely, infused with the essence of who he was becoming. He sang about uncertainty and clarity, about love lost and love found within oneself. Each note resonated with a newfound strength.

The process of recording was cathartic, allowing him to reflect on his journey. He thought of Isha often during this time—not with bitterness, but with gratitude for the love they had shared and the lessons it had taught him. He recognized that their paths had diverged, and that was okay. He could hold onto the memories while still moving forward.

As the album took shape, Abhendra began to feel a sense of purpose and identity solidify. He realized that he was not just a musician but a storyteller—a person with a narrative worth sharing.

The day came when he decided to announce the upcoming album. He sat down to write a heartfelt message to his fans, expressing his gratitude for their support during his journey. He wanted them to know that the music he was about to share was not just a collection of songs; it was a piece of his soul, an exploration of identity, and a testament to resilience.

"Hey everyone! I'm excited to announce that I'll be releasing a new album soon. It's been a challenging year, but I've used this time to reflect and explore who I am beyond just music. This album is a journey through my heart—my struggles, my growth, and my discovery of self. I can't wait to share it with you all!"

As he hit send, Abhendra felt a rush of emotions—excitement, fear, and a deep sense of relief. This was a pivotal moment in his life, a chance to redefine who he was and to embrace the complexity of his journey.

In the weeks leading up to the album release, Abhendra continued to embrace new experiences. He attended art exhibitions, explored different cuisines, and connected with people from various walks of life. Each interaction enriched his understanding of the world and himself, and he felt more grounded than he had in a long time.

Then, one day, as he was taking a walk through the park, he spotted a familiar figure in the distance. It was Isha, laughing with friends, her presence lighting up the space around her. His heart raced at the sight. The moment felt surreal—an unexpected encounter that made him question everything.

He took a deep breath, debating whether to approach her. The years of hurt, healing, and introspection culminated in this moment, and he had to decide whether he wanted to reconnect with the past or let it remain a cherished memory.

As he walked closer, he felt a mixture of hope and anxiety. What would he say? Would they pick up where they left off, or had time and circumstance changed everything?

In that split second, Abhendra realized he wasn't just approaching Isha; he was approaching a piece of himself that he had long grappled with. Whether the meeting brought closure or a new beginning, he knew it would be part of his journey of self-discovery.

With each step, he felt a surge of courage. *Who am I?* he thought. I am more than my past. I am a blend of experiences, a tapestry of connections, and a seeker of truth. And maybe, just maybe, it was time to explore the next chapter of that journey.

"The journey to finding yourself is never linear; it's a path scattered with questions and self-doubt."

– Abhendra Rathod

CHAPTER:12 REBIRTH

Healing from the Past

As the sun rose over the horizon, casting a golden glow across the city, Abhendra stood on the balcony of his apartment, reflecting on the journey that had brought him to this moment. The world below buzzed with life, a reminder of the vibrant tapestry of experiences that had shaped him. The past—filled with heartache, discovery, and growth—had forged a new version of himself. He felt a sense of rebirth, a transformation that had not only elevated his career but had also deepened his understanding of love and connection.

In the months following the release of his album, Abhendra experienced an overwhelming wave of support and appreciation. His songs resonated with people across the globe, touching hearts and igniting conversations about love, loss, and resilience. He had become an internet sensation, his music shared widely on social media platforms, each new release greeted with excitement and anticipation. Yet, amidst the accolades and fame, he remained grounded, acutely aware of the journey that had led him here.

Every note he played, every lyric he wrote, was imbued with the lessons he had learned along the way. The heartbreak he had endured was no longer a weight he carried; it had become a source of strength. He understood now that everything had happened for a reason, that every challenge had been a stepping stone toward the person he was becoming.

As he prepared for an upcoming performance at a music festival, he took a moment to breathe in the crisp morning air. The stage awaited him, but more importantly, so did the opportunity to share his story with the world. He had transformed his pain into art, and now it was time to celebrate that rebirth.

"Abhendra! You ready?" Ketan called from inside, snapping him from his reverie.

"Yeah, just taking a moment," he replied, stepping back into the warmth of the apartment.

"Good! You're going to crush it tonight. The crowd is pumped to see you!" Ketan's enthusiasm was infectious, and Abhendra felt a thrill of anticipation.

The festival grounds were alive with energy, a sea of people gathered to celebrate music and connection. As Abhendra took the stage, the roar of the crowd washed over him like a wave. The lights illuminated the sea of faces, and in that moment, he felt an exhilarating sense of belonging. This was more than just a performance; it was a celebration of life, of healing, and of the journey that had led him here.

He launched into his opening song, *Aesthetic Boy*, the crowd singing along, their voices blending with his in a powerful chorus. With each strum of the guitar, he felt the past fall away, leaving behind only the present—the joy of sharing his art and the connection he felt with his audience.

In between songs, he shared snippets of his journey, recounting the challenges and triumphs that had shaped him. "You know, a year ago, I was lost. I didn't know who I was or what I wanted. But through the struggle, I found my voice, and I found myself," he said, the words resonating deeply with those listening.

As he continued to perform, he looked out into the crowd and saw a familiar face—Sophia, a talented artist he had met during his explorations of new experiences. They had connected over their shared passion for creativity, and their friendship had blossomed into something deeper. She had become a beacon of support and understanding in his life, someone who embraced him fully, flaws and all.

Sophia's smile lit up the stage, and Abhendra felt a rush of warmth. In her presence, he had discovered a new kind of love—one built on mutual respect, shared dreams, and an understanding of each other's journeys. It was different from what he had experienced with Isha; it was grounded in friendship, trust, and the freedom to be wholly themselves.

After finishing his set, Abhendra stepped off the stage, adrenaline coursing through him. As he made his way through the crowd, he felt a sense of fulfillment that was both exhilarating and humbling. The love and support he had received from fans and friends filled him with gratitude.

"Hey! You were amazing!" Sophia exclaimed as he reached her, wrapping him in a warm embrace.

"Thanks! It felt incredible up there," he replied, his heart swelling with joy.

They found a quieter spot amidst the festival chaos, and Abhendra took a moment to gaze at Sophia. "You know, I wouldn't be here without you. You've been such an important part of my journey."

Sophia smiled softly, her eyes reflecting understanding and admiration. "You've done this all yourself, Abhendra. You took the pain and turned it into something beautiful. I'm just glad I could be here to witness your rebirth."

Their conversation flowed easily, touching on dreams, aspirations, and the future. For the first time in a long time, Abhendra felt truly at peace with himself. He understood that healing was not a linear process; it was a series of ebbs and flows, a journey that required patience and self-compassion.

As the festival continued, they wandered through the stalls, sampling food and enjoying the atmosphere. Abhendra marveled at the way his life had transformed— how he had gone from a place of despair to standing in the light of his accomplishments and newfound love.

That evening, as the sun set and the sky turned shades of pink and orange, Abhendra and Sophia found a quiet spot to watch the festivities from afar. The glow of the lights below created a magical ambiance, and he felt a profound sense of gratitude wash over him.

"I used to think love was about grand gestures and passion," Abhendra said, glancing at Sophia. "But now I see it differently. It's about companionship, respect, and understanding each other's journeys."

Sophia nodded, her gaze steady. "Exactly. It's about being there for one another, lifting each other up as you grow."

As they sat together, Abhendra felt a warmth spreading through him. This was what rebirth looked like—a reawakening of the heart and spirit. He had learned to love again, not just in the romantic sense, but in every aspect of his life. He cherished his friendships, his art, and the love he had for himself.

With each passing day, he embraced his identity as an artist, a healer, and now a partner. He had grown into a man who respected his past, understood his worth, and was ready to face the future. The shadows of his past no longer haunted him; instead, they served as reminders of how far he had come.

Achieving Success and Finding True Love

As the festival wound down and the stars began to twinkle overhead, Abhendra turned to Sophia, a sense of determination in his heart. "I want to keep creating, keep sharing my story, and keep growing. Together, let's explore the world and all its possibilities."

Sophia beamed, her eyes bright with excitement. "I'm all in. Let's create something beautiful together."

In that moment, surrounded by the magic of the festival and the promise of new beginnings, Abhendra felt an overwhelming sense of hope. He had found his voice, his purpose, and his true love. The past had shaped him, but it would not define him. He was ready for whatever came next, embracing the journey of rebirth with open arms.

As the years went by, Abhendra found true salvation from the pain and suffering that had once consumed him. He learned that healing wasn't just about moving on; it was about acknowledging the hurt and using it as a catalyst for growth. Every challenge he faced had fortified him, adding layers to his character that he had never imagined.

The scars he bore were no longer signs of vulnerability; they were badges of honor, markers of a journey well-traveled. His experiences made him more empathetic, allowing him to connect with his audience on a profound level. With each song he wrote, he wove the threads of his past into a tapestry of resilience and hope.

Abhendra had transformed his life into something that not only inspired others but also fulfilled him deeply. He recognized that everything—every heartbreak, every moment of despair—had shaped the artist he had become. In embracing his past, he found strength and purpose, and in that, he discovered the true meaning of rebirth.

"From the ashes of the past, we rise again, reborn into who we were always meant to be." – Abhendra Rathod

CONCLUSION

Reflections on Healing

Abhendra's journey through heartbreak and self-discovery resonates deeply, illustrating the complex tapestry of human emotions. His story is a compelling reminder of how love, loss, and the process of healing shape us into who we are meant to become.

From the moment he experienced the pangs of unrequited love for Isha, Abhendra was thrust into a whirlwind of emotions that tested his very essence. The pain of watching Isha move on without him ignited a fire within, one that fueled his passion for music but also left him feeling lost and isolated. Yet, it was through this struggle that he began to understand the transformative power of pain.

As he navigated the depths of despair, Abhendra gradually learned to channel his heartache into his art. His music became a sanctuary, allowing him to explore and articulate feelings that words alone could not capture. The creative process served as both a coping mechanism and a means of connection, not just with himself but with others who resonated with his experiences.

With time, he transitioned from a heartbroken young man to a celebrated artist, gaining recognition for his authenticity and emotional depth. The adoration he received from fans was a double-edged sword; while it brought him joy, it also served as a reminder of his past—a past that he had to confront and ultimately embrace.

His journey was not linear; it was filled with moments of doubt and reflection. The shift from a place of pain to one of healing was gradual, marked by setbacks and revelations. In the solitude that followed his initial success, he grappled with the question of identity. Who was he without the pain of Isha? Who was he in the light of newfound fame?

Through these trials, Abhendra emerged stronger and more self-aware. He realized that every experience—good or bad—was a necessary part of his growth. The wounds of his past, instead of defining him, became badges of honor, symbols of his resilience. He discovered that the love he had for Isha, while significant, was not the only love that could fill his life.

Insights on the Journey Through Pain to Strength

As he entered a new chapter, one marked by a renewed sense of purpose, Abhendra began to attract not just admiration but also genuine connections. He found himself surrounded by people who appreciated him for who he was, not just for his music. This newfound love—a connection that felt authentic and unburdened—opened his heart in ways he had never anticipated.

Rebirth is not merely a tale of recovering from heartbreak; it's a narrative about the beauty of transformation. Abhendra's journey teaches us that healing is not just about moving on; it's about integrating our experiences, learning from them, and using them as stepping stones toward a richer, more fulfilling life.

In the end, this book serves as a beacon of hope. It invites readers to reflect on their own experiences with love and loss, encouraging them to embrace their journeys, no matter how painful. It reassures us that every ending holds the promise of a new beginning and that through the process of healing, we can emerge stronger, wiser, and more in tune with ourselves.

Abhendra's story is a celebration of life—an affirmation that while we may be shaped by our past, we are not defined by it. It reminds us that the essence of who we are lies in our ability to rise, to create, and to love again.

"In the silence of heartbreak, you find pieces of yourself you never knew existed."

—Abhendra Rathod

BONUS POEMS

1. Shattered Echoes

There's a crack in the ceiling I can't stop staring at.

It runs the length of this apartment,

like the fault lines we ignored,

pretending love was a sturdy thing.

The whiskey's cheap, the ashtray full.

Your ghost lingers in the folds of the couch,

where we used to waste hours—

laughing, fighting,

losing ourselves between breaths.

Now it's quiet,

except for the sound of this pen,

scraping paper like it can save me.

2. Silent Storms

You left a pair of shoes by the door.

They're still there, collecting dust,

like they're waiting for you to come back

and fill them.

The nights are long,

but the mornings are worse.

I drink my coffee black now—

milk feels like too much hope.

It's funny how silence

can sound like a scream

when you're the one left behind.

3. The Weight of Goodbyes

I keep your goodbye folded in my wallet,

next to crumpled receipts

for dinners I ate alone.

It's greasy, torn at the edges,

but I can't throw it away.

Every word you said that night

is a cigarette I can't quit.

They burn slow,

but they don't kill fast enough.

Love doesn't break you;

it wears you down—

like water carving stone,

slow, inevitable, final.

4. The Void Within

I woke up to your absence again,

and it felt like being hit by a car

in slow motion.

The coffee machine sputtered;

the faucet leaked;

the world kept spinning,

but I didn't.

I tried filling the void with music,

with strangers, with alcohol.

None of it worked.

The void laughs at me now,

like it knows it's won.

Some days, I almost laugh back.